Hoaxes

by Judith Herbst

Lerner Books • London • New York • Minneapolis

First published in the United Kingdom in 2009 by
Lerner Books,
Dalton House,
60 Windsor Avenue,
London SW19 2RR

Website address: www.lernerbooks.co.uk

This edition was updated and edited for UK publication by Discovery Books Ltd.,
First Floor, 2 College Street, Ludlow, Shropshire SY8 1AN

British Library Cataloguing in Publication Data

 Herbst, Judith
   Hoaxes. - 2nd ed. - (The unexplained)
   1. Impostors and imposture - Juvenile literature
   2. Curiosities and wonders - Juvenile literature
   I. Title
   001.9'5

   ISBN-13: 978 0 7613 4309 7

Printed in Singapore

Table of Contents

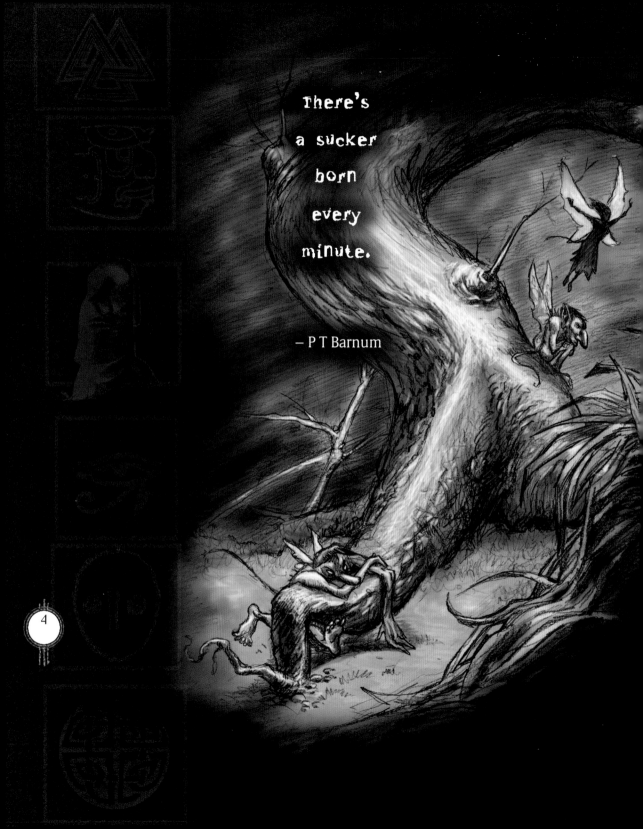

There's
a sucker
born
every
minute.

– P T Barnum

4

CHAPTER 1

SHERLOCK HOLMES IS DECEIVED

Our first story is an English fairy tale.

It is the merry month of May 1917. Sir Arthur Conan Doyle, creator of the great fictional detective Sherlock Holmes, receives a letter from a friend. The letter says that actual photographs have been taken of fairies and gnomes. Doyle gasps. He has been enchanted by this subject for quite some time and could not be more delighted by the news. Ever since he became convinced that the dead can communicate with the living, he has been a regular at séances. Now it seems that there is evidence showing that fairies are real. His eyes twinkle, and he immediately hires Edward Gardner to investigate. He should have hired Holmes.

Edward Gardner is a follower of a strange religion called theosophy. Theosophy is a mystical open house for ghosts, pixies and all things strange. Asking Gardner to investigate the fairy photographs is like sending a woodworm into a woodyard. Nevertheless, off he goes. A short time later, Doyle receives a parcel in the post. It contains two photographs.

To us, these pictures look more fake than chocolate money, mostly because

FAIRIES

Fairies are said to be small, supernatural beings who live in an enchanted land. They are usually green, wear green clothes and can make themselves invisible. Most fairies are gentle little things, but some are evil and should be avoided at all costs.

The concept of the fairy is old. Throughout the centuries, people have claimed to have had fairy encounters. Usually these encounters take place in a forest, where people are walking alone at night. Fairies seem to be part of an alternate universe, a land of make-believe that we glimpse if we are lucky or in the right place at the right time.

Frances Griffiths *(above)* and Elsie Wright *(right)* pose with their fairy friends.

the subject matter is rather suspect, but Doyle practically swoons. Gardner's enclosed letter informs Doyle that the photographers are 10-year-old Frances Griffiths and her 16-year-old cousin, Elsie Wright.

The camera they used was a Midg Quarter that exposed the image onto a glass plate (instead of film). The exposure time (how long the camera lense stays open to record the image) was 1/50th of a second. Modern cameras can take pictures much faster than that, but in those days, 1/50th of a second was considered, as Gardner described it, instantaneous. Elsie's father had loaded the camera and the girls had taken it to Cottingley Glen, a small valley where they said they often played with fairies, pixies and gnomes.

BE CAREFUL
WHAT YOU WISH FOR

The best part of any séance is when the spirits of the deceased materialize out of thin air, helped along by a medium. In July 1960, two psychic researchers, Tom O'Neill and Andrija Puharich, tried to capture one of these spirit materializations on film. With the permission of medium Edith Stillwell, they brought an army night-vision scope and an infrared camera to one of Stillwell's séances.

The room was darkened, Stillwell went into her medium routine, O'Neill's camera rolled and Puharich peered through his scope. But instead of ghosts, Puharich saw Stillwell's helpers, wearing white chiffon, sneak in through a hidden door. The film confirmed it. The spiritualists had unmasked themselves.

Doyle is very excited. He shows the pictures to his friend, Sir Oliver Lodge. Lodge is a respected physicist who had started going to séances after the death of his youngest son. If anybody would be receptive to pictures of fairies, it would likely be Lodge. However, despite his ghostly beliefs, Lodge is not impressed and expresses considerable doubt about the authenticity of the photos. Doyle dismisses Lodge, insisting that the two little girls who took the pictures came from a very good family and would hardly have known how to fake the images.

Doyle then takes the pictures to a professional photographer named Snelling, who studies them carefully. Snelling tells Doyle that there was no double exposure and that the fairies in the first photo *moved* when the shutter was snapped. He adds that he will stake his reputation on his conclusions. Doyle also enlists the help of the Kodak Company. Two experts examine the photographs and admit they can't find evidence of a trick. However, there is trouble in store.

TRICKS OF THE TRADE

Producing a fake photograph is pretty easy. In fact, in the nineteenth century, legitimate studios did it all the time. The most popular technique involved posing the subject in front of a scenic backdrop. These painted scenes were sold in rolls. Props such as columns, chairs and bookcases gave these composite pictures, as they were called, some depth.

≫ Punch, Counterpunch

The Kodak experts tell Doyle that if they spent a little time on it, they could probably produce similar pictures.

A Kodak camera sold in 1888.

9

Doyle snorts. So now, he says, the character of these little girls is being questioned! You can't find anything wrong with the photographs, so you are suggesting that just because you could create a fake picture, these children must have faked theirs!

Meanwhile, other sceptics want to know why Frances is looking directly at the camera in the first photo and *not at the fairies.* You'd think something as wondrous as a small, winged being would have captured her attention. However, Gardner counters that argument. Frances has seen fairies dozens of times, he replies, but a camera! Now that's really unusual!

The sceptics push forwards. 'You claim these girls don't have the skill to fake the pictures. Well, we happen to know Elsie has worked in a photographer's shop!'

'So what?' Gardner snaps. 'She was just an errand girl!'

The debate goes on like this for a while. Finally, Doyle announces he is going to Australia to take part in a few séances. Before he leaves, he asks Gardner to get the girls to produce more fairy pictures. Gardner promises he will try.

'My dear Sir Arthur,' Gardner writes to Doyle a short while later, 'great news! The girls have produced three more wonderful prints!'

Snelling again examines the photographs and once again proclaims the pictures genuine. 'Utterly beyond any possibility of faking!' he says, and Gardner declares the case proved. Doyle is now totally convinced that fairies exist. He writes and sends an article to the *Strand Magazine* titled, 'Fairies Photographed – An Epoch-Making Event.' This brings a hoard of

The photo of a fairy offering a flower to Elsie *(below)* is the worst of these three because the fairy looks so flat and two-dimensional – which, of course, it was.

interested journalists to the scene. With notebooks open and their pencils poised, they interview Elsie and Frances. 'Where did the fairies come from?' they ask. The girls giggle. 'We can't say.'

'OK. Then, where did the fairies go after you photographed them?' Elsie and Frances won't talk about that either. The girls refuse to discuss the matter further.

The journalists point out that the girls' behaviour is extremely suspicious, but Doyle doesn't seem to notice. He dies in 1930 firmly believing in fairies. Had it all been a hoax? No doubt about it. The girls eventually confessed, although, by that time they were well past middle age. However, despite the less-than-forceful protests of a few sceptics, a lot of people had been deceived by the fake photos. How?

≫ Paper, Scissors, Pins

Doyle was hugely popular. The public loved Sherlock Holmes' icy genius and logical mind. So if the pictures were good enough for the greatest

Scottish author Sir Arthur Conan Doyle. The analytical and highly sceptical Sherlock Holmes might have been disappointed in his gullible creator.

detective of all time, they must be the real thing. But Doyle was not Sherlock Holmes. He was the *author* of Sherlock Holmes. If anything, he was probably more like the rather dull-witted Dr Watson. (Doyle had earned his medical degree but turned to writing when his practice floundered.) Doyle's skill lay in creating plots, not in solving real mysteries. Doyle was also very gullible. He had allowed himself to be taken in by spirit mediums and if he was willing to accept visiting ghosts, why not pixies and gnomes?

A BELIEVER UNTIL THE VERY END

When Sir Arthur Conan Doyle died at the age of 81, the spiritualist community turned out in full force to rejoice. Their most famous member had passed over to the other side. Would he send them a message from beyond the grave? A week later, thousands packed a London concert hall for a grand séance. Doyle did not disappoint. Medium Estelle Roberts claimed to have established contact with the dear departed Sir Arthur.

Being a theosophist, Edward Gardner already embraced a lot of mystical ideas, so fooling him was easy. As far as the experts are concerned, some did say the pictures were suspect from the very beginning. Snelling put his seal of approval on them, but he wasn't an expert at spotting faked photographs. He was a professional photographer and the two are not the same at all.

To make matters even worse, nobody was given the correct information about the pictures. For example, Gardner said the shutter speed was 1/50th of a second, but it was probably closer to two seconds or the image wouldn't have registered. Photographic plates needed fairly long exposure times.

13

If the shutter was open for two seconds and the fairies were moving, their image would have been a blur.

Another example of incorrect information has to do with the lighting in the photographs. The first picture was supposedly taken in full sunlight, but Frances' face is clearly in shadow. Knowing the lighting, the distance between the camera and subject, the type of film used and so on is important when you are trying to determine if a picture has been faked.

Many years after Doyle and company were deceived, William Spaulding ran a computer analysis on the five fairy photographs. (The analysis was similar to the treatment given to suspicious UFO photos.) What the computer did was compare the known human figures – Elsie and Frances – to the fairy figures to see if they have the same three-dimensionality. It was hardly a surprise to learn that the fairies were only two-dimensional. In other words, they weren't real beings. What, then, were they?

Dancing fairies from *Princess Mary's Gift Book* inspired Elsie and Frances.

Elsie (*left*), said her mother in 1920, 'was a most imaginative child, who has been in the habit of drawing fairies for years'. What more can we say?

On page 14 is an illustration for a poem by Alfred Noyes titled, 'A Spell for a Fairy'. The poem appeared in *Princess Mary's Gift Book,* published in 1915. Do the little fairies look familiar to you?

We now make scissors, wire and hat pins available to the playful and somewhat mischievous Elsie Wright and Frances Griffiths. We give the girls a camera, one that they know how to use with some degree of skill. We leave them alone for a while. A spirited imagination does the rest and the gullible are invited to enjoy the results.

CHAPTER 2
GIANTS IN THE EARTH

Our next story made headlines. It actually began in 1866, but we will jump ahead to 1869. That's when the real interest started.

Stub Newell, a farmer in upstate New York, USA, has hired some men to dig a well behind his barn. It is a bright, crisp day in early autumn and the men are making good progress. Suddenly, one of the shovels clangs loudly.

'Sounds like you've hit a rock.'

The men continue to dig and quickly realize that the object they have uncovered is no ordinary stone. It is a human being. A very big human being. Wow! Maybe not a human being at all! A giant, 3 metres tall at least. What's more, it's petrified – turned completely to stone!

>> Step Right Up, Ladies and Gentlemen

In the small town of Cardiff, near New York word of the giant spreads like wildfire. Newell's neighbours flock to the farm. Then the media shows up. Newell erects a tent over his giant and starts charging money for a 15-minute look. One after another, they come, they pay, they look. Newell is making money fast. In just one day he made $1,300.

The Cardiff giant, more than 3 m in length and weighing more than one tonne, was discovered buried in the ground in Cardiff, New York, USA, in 1869.

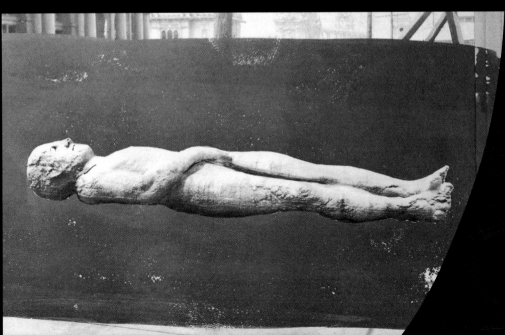

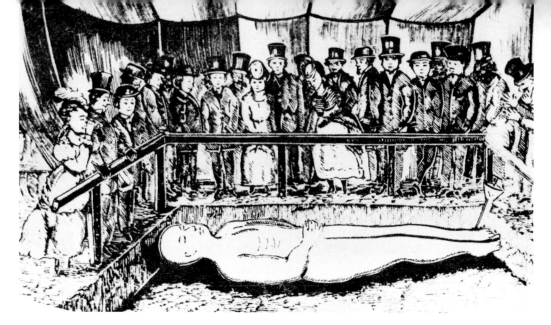

The Cardiff giant became an overnight sensation, drawing crowds from across the United States to view the find.

'What is it?' the spectators whisper, awed by the giant's imposing frame.

'He must have been in the ground a mighty long time. Look at how stained that stone is.'

The crowd leans forwards. Yes, they can see the stains.

'I feel,' breathes one man, 'that I'm in the presence of a great and superior being.' A woman beside him nods respectfully.

'There were giants in the earth in those days,' someone mumbles and the crowd is hushed.

Could this be a member of the race of giants that the Bible talks about in Genesis? What a find that would be! It would mean all the legends are true!

The scientific community quickly learns of the Cardiff giant. Some of the esteemed scientists rub their beards and nod. They are convinced that a body can be turned into stone if the conditions are right. Others rub their beards and shake their heads. 'This is not', they say, 'a human being at all, but a statue. Very ancient, no doubt.' Still others, like Andrew White of Cornell University, Ithaca, USA, don't rub their beards at all. 'Poppycock!' they shout. 'The thing's fake!'

Local newspapers in Cardiff and surrounding villages are enchanted and cover the story with great energy. There is no need to check the facts, they all decide. Cardiff is booming. Business is great. Out of town newspapers, however, are determined to dig up the truth.

>> A Scheme Hatches

Our story now flashes back three years. George Hull, cigar maker and scoundrel, is looking for a money making scheme. A conversation with a travelling preacher gives him an idea. Two years later, on 5 June 1868, he travels to Fort Dodge, Iowa, where he knows there are gypsum quarries. He hires a man to cut out a 3.5 m by 1.5 m block, 55 centimetres thick. Hull then ships the stone block to Chicago. There, two sculptors he has hired carve the block into the shape of a man. Hull knows his petrified man has to look real, so he attaches long, thick

George Hull is pictured here with his creation.

needles to a block of wood and pounds the sculpture to give it pores. He ages it with wet sand, ink and sulphuric acid. As he stands back to take a look at his creation, a smile plays across his lips. Ahhh, perfect!

Hull has a cousin in upstate New York, named Stub Newell. He knows good old Stub will go along with his little hoax, especially since there will be money in it for him. So Hull moves the stone giant east by train and then hauls it the last few kilometres on a wagon under the cover of night. Two weeks after it arrives, Hull and Newell bury the giant behind Newell's barn. A year later, its discovery explodes across the front pages of newspapers all around the country.

Two weeks into the hoax, Hull decides it's time to get out. He sells three-quarters of his stake in the giant to a group of businessmen for $30,000. By now, the Cardiff giant has been exposed as the Cardiff fake, but the public doesn't care. The giant goes on a whirlwind tour of the country, finally

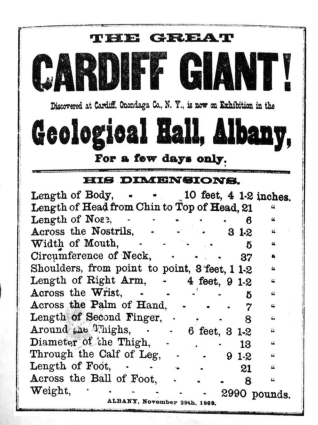

THE GREAT

CARDIFF GIANT!

Discovered at Cardiff, Onondaga Co., N. Y., is now on Exhibition in the

Geological Hall, Albany,

For a few days only.

HIS DIMENSIONS.

Length of Body,	10 feet, 4 1-2 inches.
Length of Head from Chin to Top of Head,	21 "
Length of Nose,	6 "
Across the Nostrils,	3 1-2 "
Width of Mouth,	5 "
Circumference of Neck,	37 "
Shoulders, from point to point,	3 feet, 1 1-2 "
Length of Right Arm,	4 feet, 9 1-2 "
Across the Wrist,	5 "
Across the Palm of Hand,	7 "
Length of Second Finger,	8 "
Around the Thighs,	6 feet, 3 1-2 "
Diameter of the Thigh,	13 "
Through the Calf of Leg,	9 1-2 "
Length of Foot,	21 "
Across the Ball of Foot,	8 "
Weight,	2990 pounds.

ALBANY, November 29th, 1869.

The Cardiff giant appeared 'for a few days only' at Geological Hall in Albany, New York. The hoax became a great money maker for its perpetrator.

20

ending up in the Farmers' Museum in Cooperstown, New York. And as for Mr Hull . . . ?

It is early autumn 1877. William Conant and his son are walking just outside the village of Beulah, Colorado, when they notice something strange sticking out of the ground. They kneel down, scrape away some of the soil and realize it is a man's foot. Further digging reveals a stony, human-like creature, 2.5 m tall, with a small head and exceptionally long arms. Newspapers rush to the scene. Could this be, they ask breathlessly, the missing link between humans and apes that scientists have been searching for?

Or could it be one more scheme by Mr George Hull?

CHAPTER 3
RAINFOREST SHADINESS

Our third story takes place in the jungle. It has everything you could ever want – suffocating humidity, poisonous snakes, mosquitoes the size of aeroplanes and a lost tribe of primitive people. The story begins in 1971.

'Come closer,' says the man who calls himself Dafal. His dark eyes twinkle with a secret. He is a member of the Blit Manubo tribe on Mindanao, one of the islands that makes up the country called the Philippines. He knows many things.

Manuel Elizalde Jr leans forward, curious and alert.

'Not far away,' Dafal says, pointing off into the trees, 'there is a tribe. Very small. Very primitive. The people live in caves. They have no agriculture and no weapons. They have no domesticated animals. They use only the simplest tools.' Dafal spreads his fingers. They are long and graceful. 'These people,' he continues, 'have lived this way for centuries, hidden from the world. No one but me knows they are there. Except you, Elizalde, now you know.'

Well, Elizalde is not about to keep this quiet. He rushes back to Manila and hands the story to the newspapers. Before anyone knows what's happening, the country is crawling with anthropologists. One after the other, they make their way into the steamy Mindanao rainforest. Local guides are more than happy to show them the way to the little lost tribe. The anthropologists gape. They stare. They take pictures and make notes. 'This is amazing!' they all say. 'These people are still living in the Stone Age.'

The Tasaday, as the tribe is called, wear loincloths and skirts made of orchid leaves. They have only scrapers, axes, digging sticks and drills for making fire. They subsist on whatever they can find in the forest – palm fruit, wild bananas, wild yams, crabs, small fish, grubs and frogs. They have lived this way for centuries, isolated and primitive, a group of 26 people suspended in time. The anthropologists have to pinch themselves. They can't believe it.

>> Paleohippies Meet the World

Within days, it seems, there is a helicopter flying over the forest. The churning air shakes the trees and sends dirt and stones scattering. Heads tilt upwards to watch the strange craft touch down on Mindanao. Even before the blades settle to stillness, the door opens and out jumps a team from the *National Geographic* magazine, dressed in khakis and weighted down with camera equipment.

When the pictures appear in *National Geographic*'s August 1972 issue, they seem like stills from a film. Nearly naked people sit, as if posed, on rocky outcrops. Their soft, brown faces stare blankly at the camera, their lives rudely invaded. *Who are you?* they seem to be saying. We are the world.

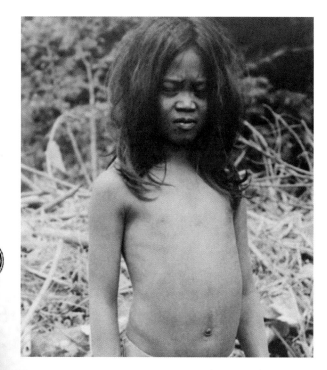

A Tasaday boy

The *National Geographic* story is spellbinding. Readers are enchanted by the simplicity and serenity of the Tasaday. One anthropologist playfully calls them 'paleohippies'. Everyone has adopted them, and NBC (National Broadcasting Company), from the USA, gives Elizalde $50,000 to make a documentary about them. Scholars begin to

Two of the original Tasaday, Lolo and Bilengan *(left and centre)*, were photographed with Datu' Galang *(right)*, a Tboli leader, in 1999.

study their language. Others write books. And then, just like that, the whole dizzying Tasaday roller coaster screeches to a halt. On 21 September 1972, a corrupt President Ferdinand Marcos declares martial law and the Philippines suddenly becomes off limits to foreigners.

For 14 years, nothing is heard from or about the Tasaday. As suddenly as they appeared, they vanished. However, in 1986, Marcos is thrown out of power. There is a new government. The Philippines is open once again. Anxious for another close-up look at the Tasaday, Swiss journalist Oswald Iten returns to Mindanao. He hikes through the rainforest, slashing at the overgrowth with a machete. When he reaches the forest caves, he finds them empty. Hello? Anybody home?

25

➤➤ You Can't Hide Much in a Pair of Shorts

A shocked Iten does a little investigation and discovers the shy, primitive, Stone Age Tasaday walking around in shorts and T-shirts. They have blended in with Blit Manubo and Tboli tribes and are growing crops, living in huts and sleeping on wooden beds! Iten knows a scam when he

Experts had questioned how the rainforest, which doesn't produce much food fit for humans, could have supported people who didn't also rely on agriculture.

sees one and announces to the Tasaday that the game is up. 'Come clean,' he says. 'Tell me what's going on here.'

With a little coaxing, a few of the Tasaday confess that the whole thing had been Elizalde's idea. He had asked them to pretend that they were a long-lost primitive tribe.

Why? Iten wants to know.

The actors shrug. They don't know. Maybe to fool people. Just for fun. The only people having fun would have been Elizalde and the Marcos government. Their plan was to give the world an intriguing mystery that would quickly line their pockets. Deep in the heart of the Philippine jungle, they told everyone, a small group of people remains frozen in time. These cave dwellers are from another age, so far away that there are no memories of it. They speak their own language and know nothing of the world that has grown up around them. They are strange and exotic, a lost tribe, just like in films. Upon hearing about this tribe, the anthropologists would descend like flies. Soon there would be TV coverage, publicity, money! The Philippine government would take over the 'Tasaday' forestlands and eventually turn them into private profits for the already bloated Marcos regime. It was the perfect scheme.

Except, of course, it wasn't. Several anthropologists had already begun to suspect that something was not right about the Tasaday. How had such a small group of individuals survived for so long? Why hadn't they died out? The anthropologists also questioned the Tasaday's food source, which was essentially the rainforest itself. Despite how lush it appears, the rainforest would not provide enough food to adequately nourish a human being. All the other tribes who live on the island of Mindanao supplement their diet with crops that they grow.

When all was said and done, nobody really had much fun after all. President Marcos died in exile, Elizalde never made the money he had hoped for and the anthropologists went home with nothing except mosquito bites, but maybe the Tasaday had a good time. Everybody wants to be famous.

CHAPTER 4
THE *SUN*, THE MOON AND BATMAN

Now for a little science fiction.

It is August 1835, and so far there are only seven known planets in the solar system. Still, astronomy is making progress. Telescopes are getting bigger and producing sharper images, and scientists are finding things they never dreamed existed. Life, they believe, is everywhere. No one has proved this yet, of course, but it makes perfect sense. How can Earth be the only inhabited planet in such a vast universe? The British astronomer Sir William Herschel has come out in favour of life on the Moon, the planets and possibly even the Sun. Others echo his confidence. The time is ripe for a hoax.

≫ The Pen Is Mightier than the Truth

Enter, now, our hero – or perhaps, our villain, depending on your point of view. He is Richard Locke, journalist for the *Sun*, a newspaper in New York City, USA. When Locke joins the staff, the two-year-old *Sun* is struggling to survive in a field of older, more established newspapers. Locke knows that if the *Sun* folds, he will be out of a job. So he decides that what the paper needs is a hot story that will boost readership and keep him eating his three meals a day.

The *Sun* breaks the story about life on the Moon.

Locke pitches his hot story idea to his publisher. The publisher gives him the go-ahead. 'Sure, try it,' he murmurs. So Locke puts on his thinking cap. In no time at all, Locke is seized with an idea. His eyes twinkle mischievously. 'Oooo,' he says, or words to that effect. Grinning, he sits down at his desk, dunks his pen into a pot of ink and begins to write.

It is early morning on 25 August. An orange sun rises in the sky. The city's newspapers hit the streets with a thud. The *Sun* hits the streets and leaves a crater. A banner headline shrieks the news: LIFE DISCOVERED ON MOON! The *Sun* sells out completely.

The basis for this remarkable story is supposedly the secretly obtained results of Sir John Herschel's expedition to the Cape of Good Hope, Africa.

According to Richard Locke, astronomer Sir John Herschel (*right*) described in great detail what he observed as life on the Moon.

An artist rendered this illustration of the Moon based on Locke's accounts in the *Sun*.

Sir John, an astronomer, has gone off to catalogue stars in the Southern Hemisphere. But, according to the *Sun,* he has also been looking at the Moon and planets though a gigantic telescope he has built. What do you think he's seen? A lively Moon, that's what! There are forests up there and deep rivers and smooth, sandy beaches. Most extraordinary of all, the *Sun* reports, are the Moon's creatures. In his most flowing writing style, Locke enthusiastically describes 'herds of brown quadrupeds' and gunmetal-blue antelopes. There are also unicorns and humanlike beavers, which have discovered fire and live in well constructed huts.

The *Sun*'s readers are breathless. Naturally they want to know more, so Locke writes part two of the story. It's published the following day. Locke is doing really well now. His clever mixture of fact, fantasy and seasoned newspaper savvy is selling papers so fast, that the printing presses can hardly keep up. By the third installment, readers are practically dribbling. Letters pour into the *Sun*'s offices. Everyone wants to know if there are people on the Moon. Readership is soaring. No one else is carrying the story. (You know why.) It's the greatest scoop of all time! The publisher of the *Sun* is dancing on the desks. 'Go ahead!' he shouts gleefully to Locke. 'Tell them more about the Moon people!'

≫ All This and Batman Too.

In the fourth installment, Locke delivers. The Moon, he reveals to thousands of panting readers, is inhabited by man-bats. Their scientific name is *Verspertilio homo.* The man-bats are about 1.2 m high and they are covered with short, reddish hair. Their huge wings extend from the

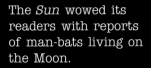

The *Sun* wowed its readers with reports of man-bats living on the Moon.

top of their shoulders to their calves and, when they are not walking upright, they soar effortlessly through the lunar air. Their faces resemble that of the orangutan, but they are very humanlike in their expressions. (All this Herschel is supposedly seeing through a telescope.)

August melts into September, and the installments keep coming. Newspapers up and down the East Coast actually applaud the *Sun's* handling of the story. Even the *New York Times* is impressed and calls the reports 'probable and plausible.' But wait. It gets even more bizarre.

One afternoon, Locke looks up from his desk and sees two gentlemen.

'Mr Locke?'

Our hero nods.

'I am Professor Dennison Olmstead and this is my colleague Professor Elias Loomis. We're from Yale University.'

Locke knows what's coming but remains composed. He politely extends his hand.

'We are most anxious,' says Olmstead, 'to have a look at those lunar calculations.'

'Uh, yes,' says Locke. He pushes out a smile.

The *Sun,* it seems, has been telling its readers that it has proof of all the lunacy it's been dishing out. There are supposedly 40 pages of mathematical computations from the *Edinburgh Journal of Science* that show how all this Moon life could have developed.

GETTING YOUR MONEY'S WORTH

In the early nineteenth century, newspapers were
very dull, dealing only with political and financial news. .
In 1833, Benjamin Day, a publisher from New York,
published the first edition of the *New York Sun*, a four-page
penny newspaper (it was called a 'penny' paper, because it only
cost one penny to buy). Day believed in giving the public what
they wanted – humour, entertainment and lots of crime and
violence. The *Sun* was an instant hit. Other penny papers tried to
match Day's success and the race was on to find – or make up –
the most lurid and sensational stories possible.

Eventually, most of the penny papers folded. The *Sun*, however,
kept going even after Day sold it in 1868. However, the stories
gradually grew more conservative. In 1916, the *Sun*
merged with the *New York Press* and, a few years later,
the *Globe*. By 1950 it was all but gone, surviving
as the last two words on the front page of the
New York World-Telegram and Sun.
Eventually that, too, folded.

The *Sun* didn't print any of it because it was much too technical for the
average reader. *But these two,* Locke is now thinking, *are not the average
reader. They're scientists. Hmmm. Now what?*

Locke swallows. 'Well, Professors,' he says. 'A funny thing. The papers are
not here. If you can believe it, we sent them off to the printer not ten
minutes ago. Down the hall, turn left, take the stairs and go down two
flights, down the hall, turn right.' He adds another smile.

Off go the professors. The printer also has bad news. 'You just missed them,' he says. 'The papers were shipped out.'

The professors are again on the move and by day's end, they have toured half of New York with nothing to show for it. If they are starting to get suspicious, they keep it to themselves.

By September, Locke decides he's had enough. One of his friends at the *Journal of Commerce* is just about to reprint the story, and Locke finds he doesn't have the heart to let him go through with it. He confesses all, and the *Journal* gets a scoop on an exposé of the Great Moon Hoax. The *Sun* never apologizes.

'Who cares if we made it all up?' says its publisher. 'We sold a few papers and everybody had a good read.'

So much for responsible journalism. As for Herschel, well, he thinks the whole thing is funny and admits that his actual discoveries probably won't be half as interesting. As for the public?

Some of us still believe everything we read.

CHAPTER 5
GRAFFiTi iN tHE GRAiN

Our last story is a good old-fashioned mystery. It takes place in England, birthplace of great mysteries. The year is 1965. The place is Warminster in southern England. The night is dark but not stormy. Had there been a storm, Gordon Faulkner wouldn't have been able to get a decent photograph of the disk-shaped UFO. However, the night sky is clear and Gordon gets his snapshot.

The photograph quickly makes its way into the tabloid newspapers and triggers a rash of UFO sightings. Everyone in Warminster, it seems, is seeing lights in the sky. Night after night, the people gather at the top

Cradle Hill and Starr Hill, the two best viewing points in town. The UFOs do not disappoint. The crowd is treated to a variety show of mysterious lights, strange shapes and eerie sounds. This goes on for quite some time, and Warminster gains the reputation of being UFO central.

» UFO Footprints?

We now jump forwards 15 years. It is a quiet day in early August 1980. A tourist has come to see Britain's famous chalk sculptures. As he walks along the earthworks, his eyes settle on a field at the foot of the hill. There, etched in the grain, are three enormous circles. The tourist blinks and blinks again. 'Well, this is certainly very curious,' he thinks. The circles are very precise and perfectly shaped and look, well . . . *wrong* in the middle of the grain. Intrigued by the mystery, the tourist phones the offices of the nearby *Wiltshire Times.* The *Wiltshire Times* is a small

Facing page: A prehistoric chalk horse carved into a hillside in Wiltshire, England. *Below:* An early crop circle, Wiltshire, 1989

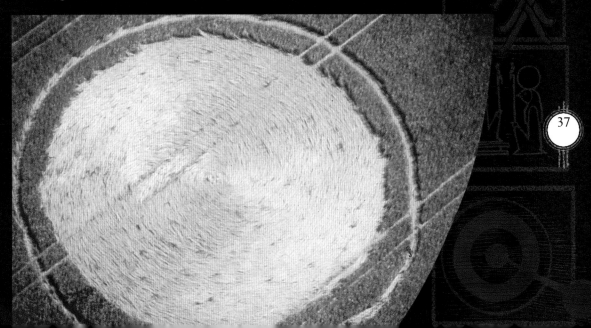

37

weekly newspaper, but it is professional in every respect. A short time later, a journalist and a photographer arrive at the scene. When the paper publishes its next edition a few days later, the eye-catching headline sets the stage.

MYSTERY CIRCLES – RETURN OF THE 'THING?'

Despite what it sounds like, the 'Thing' is not some enormous reptile that tramples cities. It is, instead, the *Times'* nickname for the legendary Warminster UFO from the 1960s. Is the paper suggesting that aliens made the circles? Well, not exactly, but the story certainly fires up people's imaginations.

UFO enthusiasts get very excited. The day after the *Times* article appears, Ian Mrzyglod, Mike Seager, Terry Chivers and Julie Blake arrive in Warminster, ready to investigate. Mrzyglod and his team are amateur researchers, but they have a keen interest in finding out

A crop circle investigator takes measurements and notes in a field.

the truth. They describe themselves as sceptical and say that they are well aware that 90 per cent of all UFO sightings turn out to be known objects. Armed with measuring tapes, cameras and plastic bags, the team of four spreads out to gather evidence.

One of the circles is in a field of winter wheat on a farm owned by Geoff Cooper. Cooper tells Mrzyglod that this is the *second* one he has found. The first circle appeared in May, but it had since been ploughed under. The other two circles are on the neighbouring farm, pressed into an oat field. The farmer says he discovered one on the morning of 21 July and the other 10 days later, also in the morning.

'Did you hear anything? See anything?' Mrzyglod asks. The two farmers shake their heads.

Cooper rubs his chin. 'But my housekeeper,' he says, 'she did. Strange humming sounds, she said they were coming from the fields. They would be on for 20 minutes and then off for 10, on for 20, off for 10. The dogs were barking, too. All night long.'

≫ Theories, Anyone?

Mrzyglod and the others can see that the grain has been flattened – not cut – and that the stalks all lie swirled in a clockwise direction. Mrzyglod suggests four possibilities. The circles were made by a UFO, a helicopter, a hoaxer or a whirlwind of some kind. The researchers get to work. They send soil and stalk samples from the three sites to a technician at Bristol University, who tests them for radioactivity. (UFO researchers seem to think that a flying saucer landing site should be radioactive.) The report comes back negative. Mrzyglod decides to set aside the UFO hypothesis for lack of any substantial proof.

Researchers were amazed that the stalks in crop circles were bent but not broken. What could have caused such results? they wondered.

Both the British Army and the Royal Aeronautical Society deny that any helicopters were in the area, so that theory is dismissed. The team also concludes that the circles probably weren't made as a hoax, mostly because nobody can find any trails through the cornstalks. A hoaxer would have had to come in with a machine of some kind and would have certainly trampled the grain. There's no sign that anything was dragged, lugged or ridden onto the field. So all that's left is the whirlwind theory.

At first, this one seems plausible. At Mrzyglod's request, Terence Meaden, an expert on tornadoes and bizarre weather, agrees to study the crop circles. He concludes that a whirlwind could certainly have created the swirling pattern. He goes on to describe low-pressure pockets and thermal updrafts. It's all very scientific and very convincing. Meaden is confident. Mrzyglod and his research team are satisfied. However, the game is just getting started.

You Can Fool a Lot of the People a Lot of the Time

The following summer, almost to the day, three more crop circles appear at a place called the Devil's Punchbowl in Surrey. This time, however, they don't look quite so 'natural'. They are strung out in a line, with the inner circle almost twice as large as the two outer ones. Meaden, puzzled by the symmetry of the design, adjusts his theory. He adds prevailing winds, leeward slopes and oncoming frontal systems.

UFO enthusiasts, meanwhile, are convinced the circles are flying saucer landing sites, called 'nests'. When the spinning disk lifts off (supposedly), circulating air flattens the grain, leaving a depression that resembles a bird's nest. If ever there was a spot for UFO nests, this part of England is certainly it!

Crop circles continued to show up in England throughout the 1980s and 1990s.

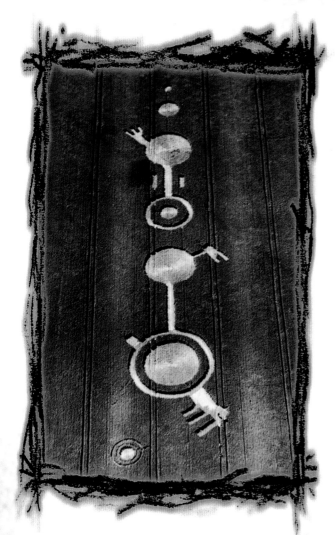

Some crop circles have very intricate patterns, such as this one that appeared in Wiltshire in 1990.

Baffled and intrigued, curious and delighted, people flock to see the crop circles. They measure them. They photograph them. They test the soil and study the crushed stalks under microscopes. The UFO enthusiasts set up viewing areas to watch for flying saucer activity. The sceptics set up night vision cameras in the hope of catching the hoaxers in the act. However, everyone is outfoxed. Summer after summer, the circles continue to appear wherever the watchers aren't. The patterns are now very stylized. Some are even starting to resemble occult symbols. 'They're messages!' breathe the UFO buffs, 'from *out there*!'

Thirteen years pass.

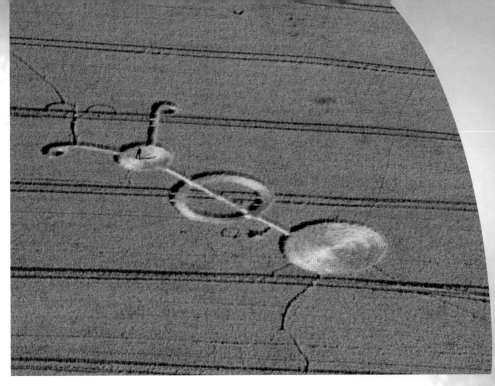

Insectograms are crop circles in the form of giant insects, such as this ant-like crop circle in Hampshire.

'Well,' Dave Chorley may have said, one late summer afternoon, 'I think I've had enough.'

Doug Bower would then have nodded. 'Yes. We're too old for this.'

'It was fun, though, wasn't it?'

'Our best prank, I'd say.'

'I thought they'd get it after we made the insectograms.'

'Pretty foolish, they were.'

Doug may have chuckled softly at the public's willingness to believe all kinds of nonsense.

So, on the morning of 4 September, Dave Chorley and Doug Bower formally confessed to a journalist. With a heavy steel bar and then

Dave Chorely and Doug Bower plot out a crop circle. Dave and Doug were the first to flatten symbols in fields, but they have inspired many other crop artists around the world.

later with planks and ropes, they had made the crop circles. In Surrey and Warminster. At Wantage and Winterbourne Stoke. At Chilcomb and near Stonehenge. No helicopters, no whirlwinds and no aliens had been involved. It had all been done by two practical jokers, now in their 60s, after a few pints of stout at the local pub.

The mystery of the crop circles was finally solved, and everyone should have been happy, except that nobody really was. The scientists had been fooled and that embarrassed them. The people who had invented the new field (no pun intended) of 'cereology' watched a source of income disappear. The UFO lovers who had thought they were finally going to make contact had their hopes dashed. So there was only one thing left to do. Ignore the confession.

Crop circles still show up every now and then. It's a strange ending to the story, but then human beings are a funny bunch. We love a good hoax. It shows enterprise and inventiveness. Even if we end up with egg on our faces, it doesn't matter. It's usually fun while it lasts and sometimes, its far more interesting than the truth.

>> Find Out More

Books

Barker, Cicely May. *The Complete Book of Flower Fairies* Frederick Warne Publishers Limited, 2002.

Coghill, Julie. *The 10 Most Outrageous Hoaxes* Franklin Watts, 2007.

Pringle, Lucy. *Crop Circles: Art in the Landscape* Frances Lincoln Children's Books, 2007.

Townsend, John. *Fakes and Forgeries* (Freestyle: True Crime) Raintree Publishers, 2005.

Woolf, Alex. *Investigating Fakes and Hoaxes* (Forensic Files) Heinneman Library, 2004.

We6sites

The Cottingley Fairies
www.cottingleyconnect.org.uk/fairies.htm
On this website you can learn more about where the fairies were found and have a look at all the pictures that Frances Griffiths and Elsie Wright took.

The Museum of Hoaxes
www.museumofhoaxes.com
This website includes a frequently updated blog of scams and practical jokes from around the world.

Films

FairyTale: A True Story. Icon Entertainment International, 1997.
This fim about the Cottingley fairies was filmed in Yorkshire, England, where the real Elsie Wright and Frances Griffiths lived. All the characters involved in the original story are featured, including the fairies.

Signs. Touchstone Pictures, 2002.
In this film, Mel Gibson plays a farmer who discovers that something very strange is happening in his cornfield. Please note, this film is rated PG-13.

≫ About the Author

Born in Baltimore, Maryland, USA, Judith Herbst grew up in Queens, New York, where she learned to jump double skipping ropes with amazing skill. She has since lost that ability. A former English teacher, she ran away from school to become a writer. Her first book for children was *Sky Above and Worlds Beyond,* whose title, she admits, was much too long. She loves to write and would rather be published, she says, than be rich, which has turned out to be the case. Herbst spends her summers in Maine on a lake with her cats and laptop.

≫ Photo·Acknowledgements

Photographs and illustrations in this book are used courtesy of: Fortean Picture Library, pp 7 (both), 11 (all), 12, 14, 15, 36, 37 (Terence Meaden), 38 (Dr G T Meaden), 40 (Bob Skinner), 41 (Bob Skinner), 42, 44 (Robert Irving); © Bettmann/CORBIS, pp 9, 17, 18, 19, 20, 22, 24, 31, 32; © Robin Hemley, p 25; © Stephen G Donaldson Photography, p 26; © AIP Emilio Segré Visual Archives, T J J See Collection, p 30; © Christopher Cormack/CORBIS, p 43. Illustrations by © Bill Hauser/Independent Picture Service, pp 4-5, 6, 16, 28, 29.
Cover photograph by © Christopher Cormack/CORBIS